Ballerina Biker

Ballerina Biker

Robin and Chris Lawrie

Illustrated by
Robin Lawrie

Acknowledgements

The authors and publishers would like to thank Julia Francis, Hereford Diocesan Deaf Church lay co-chaplain, for her help with the sign language in the *Chain Gang* books, and Dr Cathy Turtle, ecologist, for her help with the selection of species in books 13 to 18.

Published by Evans Brothers Limited
2A Portman Mansions
Chiltern Street
London W1U 6NR

© Robin and Christine Lawrie
First published 2004

The authors assert their moral right to be identified as the authors of this work in accordance with the Copyright, Designs and Patents Act, 1988.

Printed in Hong Kong

British Library Cataloguing in Publication data.
Lawrie, Robin
  Ballerina Biker. – (The Chain Gang)
  1. Slam Duncan (Fictitious character) – Juvenile fiction
  2. All terrain cycling – Juvenile fiction 3. Adventure stories
  4. Children's stories
  I. Title II. Lawrie, Chris
  823.9'14[J]

ISBN 0 237 525615

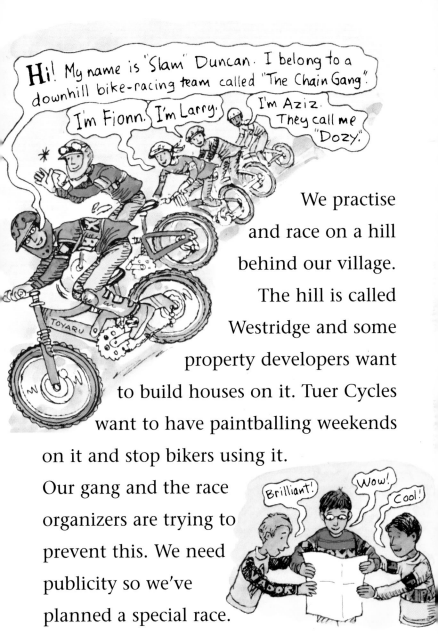

Hi! My name is "Slam" Duncan. I belong to a downhill bike-racing team called "The Chain Gang".

I'm Fionn.

I'm Larry.

I'm Aziz. They call me "Dozy".

We practise and race on a hill behind our village. The hill is called Westridge and some property developers want to build houses on it. Tuer Cycles want to have paintballing weekends on it and stop bikers using it. Our gang and the race organizers are trying to prevent this. We need publicity so we've planned a special race.

Brilliant!

Wow!

Cool!

*I'm Andy. (Andy is deaf and signs.)

5

Saturday morning the gang were all at
my house when the postman arrived.
There was a big envelope
addressed to me.
It was a poster for
our race.

Save our Hill!

WESTLAND SUPER SERIES

Presents

ROUND 2 DOWNHILL RACE

PLUS live TV coverage

of

DAD'S FANCY DRESS RACE

Whoever wins could give a speech about
saving our hill on TV. Let's make sure
it's one of our dads!

There was a parcel for my sister, too.

She had ordered some shoes on the net.

My mum didn't like them.

A typical Saturday morning, but we had

a race to practise for.

Two weeks later. Race day. We'd built a tough new North Shore-type course with ramps and elevated sections. Our timed runs down were at thirty-second intervals.

I was the last one down in my class.

I was nervous, but I was really flying –

. . . over the flyover . . .

The Dads' Fancy Dress race was going to be straight after lunch. So the queue for burgers was a strange sight!

Then I saw my arch rival, Punk Tuer, and his slimy sidekick, Dyno Sawyer, butting into the queue.

After lunch we were chilling outside the refreshment tent, waiting for the Dads' Fancy Dress race to start.

We had been counting on my dad or Larry's dad winning. They had their speeches for the save-the-hill campaign ready to deliver in front of the cameras. But Bob Turner would wipe the floor with them.

If we lost Westridge we couldn't practise. It was miles and miles to the next decent downhill course. This was serious stuff – but Larry just wasn't concentrating.

WOW! And what are you? A pearl-bordered fritillary, I'd say. Just imagine, not long ago you were an ugly little caterpillar and look at you now!

14

Too bad this doesn't always happen with humans, Larry. You're not good looking and neither is your dad.
Yeah, in fact you look a lot like each other. I bet if you put on your dad's panto costume you'd look just like him.
Can you people SHUT UP! And concentrate on how we're going to SAVE OUR HILL.
Hey! I've got a great idea!

16

We caught Larry's dad on the way out of his caravan where he had been getting dressed up. We explained our idea to him. He loved it!

Now all we had to do was get Larry *in* the caravan and dress *him* up.

It took a while but finally . . .

What a babe!

wow

Just one problem.

*Cool!

But then . . .

I got on my bike and rode home.

*That's a problem.

Luckily, Sis was out.

Back on the hill a few minutes later . . .

He gave in and headed for the start line.

It was a wonderful sight.
First away was
the gorilla
(Fionn's dad
on a rubbish bike).

Thirty seconds later it was the turn

of the astronaut
(Dozy's dad) who
was pretty good
and had actually done
some practising.

Thirty seconds after him it was
time for the stick
of celery (Andy's
dad) to get moving.

Thirty more and the cowboy (my dad)

got going. He was a
pretty fair rider and I
was worried that he'd
munch the celery!

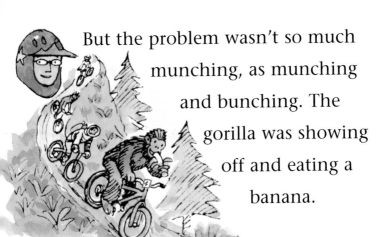

But the problem wasn't so much munching, as munching and bunching. The gorilla was showing off and eating a banana.

From where I stood I saw it all. Riding one-handed downhill is never a great idea. The other riders had all bunched up behind him so when he crashed . . .

. . . they all crashed!

21

Once the mess had been cleared up and the riders got clear of the course, it was time for Larry, or should I say Widow Twanky, to have his/her run.

But it was obvious straight away that the high heels were going to be a problem for Larry, especially with Bob Turner, alias Dyno's dad, alias 'the ballerina', breathing down his neck.

Hey, you ride pretty good for a 'dad,' don't you?

Larry had had enough of silly
high heel shoes. So he kicked
them off.

One of them flew into Bob Turner's
front wheel, jamming it solid . . .

He did a
jump that any
ballerina would have
been proud of.

And that was that. Widow Twanky didn't have much competition from the other dads and won easily.

Back in the caravan, Larry just had time to change before our afternoon runs. And his dad needed the costume for his TV interview.

On the way to the start line Fionn grabbed Larry . . .

I don't think "Pretty Peach" is really your colour.

. . . and wiped off his lippy.

Meanwhile, Bob Turner was not a happy
ballerina.

Sometimes Dozy can be VERY silly.

But inside there *was* somebody's dad –

Larry's!

He could be pretty scary, too.

Back to business. This race series looked like being the last on our hill and I wanted to win it. I'd been fastest in the morning runs but I could still lose this race if anyone went faster this afternoon.

Fortunately, Punk's dad was so furious that Bob Turner had blown the chance of free paintballing publicity that he'd taken Punk and

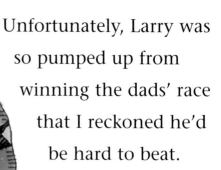

Dyno home early. Less competition.

Unfortunately, Larry was so pumped up from winning the dads' race that I reckoned he'd be hard to beat.

And I was right.

He must have felt as free as a bird without that silly panto costume on, so he did his best jumps ever and . . .

. . . his very best technical descents. Larry had never been very good on the really scary drops. But today he was unstoppable.

Another easy win.

Later, with Larry beside him on the podium,
Larry's dad gave his speech
in front of the TV cameras.

Great stuff. But then . . .

Then the WEIRDEST thing happened . . .

If I live to be 100, I'll never figure it out!